BALLOON
CARTOONS
AND OTHER FAVORITES

BALLOON CARTOONS
AND OTHER FAVORITES

AARON HSU-FLANDERS

CB
CONTEMPORARY BOOKS
CHICAGO

Hsu-Flanders, Aaron.
    Balloon cartoons and other favorites / Aaron Hsu-Flanders.
        p.   cm.
    ISBN 0-8092-3953-1 (paper)
    1. Balloon sculpture.   2. Cartoon characters.   I. Title.
TT926.H782   1991
745.594—dc20   91-20399
                                                              CIP

Line drawings by Lillian Hsu-Flanders

Published by Contemporary Books, Inc.
Two Prudential Plaza, Chicago, Illinois 60601-6790
Manufactured in the United States of America
International Standard Book Number: 0-8092-3953-1

For Lillian and Adriel

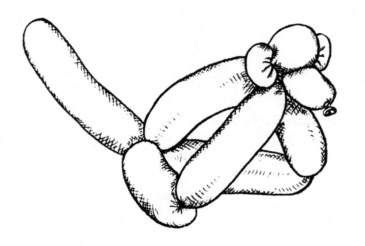

CONTENTS

ACKNOWLEDGMENTS

Special thanks are reserved for: Harvey Plotnick, my publisher, for his endless enthusiasm; Stacy Prince, my editor, for all of her creative contributions; Eric (Cheezo) Persson, a truly great clown, for his enduring camaraderie; Dr. Ivan Ciric, who saved my life many, many years ago; Alan Lewitz, who was there in the very beginning; and Larry Tribe, my friend, who tried to reverse my thinking and convince me, in his inimitable fashion, that maybe this whole balloon phenomenon had everything to do with me and nothing to do with balloons.

CAUTION:

Do *not* put inflated, tied balloons in your mouth for any reason. Even if you wish you had a few extra hands to make a certain animal, resist the temptation to hold a balloon part between your lips even for a second; if the balloon pops you could have a piece of latex forced down your throat. For this reason it is best not to let children under the age of three—who cannot help putting everything in their mouths—handle the balloons at all. Even uninflated balloons can cause choking or suffocation. Be sure to supervise any child under the age of seven who wishes to make balloon animals himself or herself.

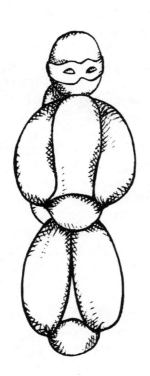

INTRODUCTION

When I was a kid, I was fascinated watching performers twist and turn a long, thin balloon until it miraculously became a dog, or a swan, or a rabbit. By age 13 I'd procured some of those special balloons for myself and I was hooked—instantly. Before long I started making balloon animals for friends, which led to my performing at parties and anywhere else people wanted to make others happy. I was having so much fun with something that was basically quite easy that I decided to share the joy and wrote *Balloon Animals*, which was followed quickly by *More Balloon Animals* and *Balloon Hats & Accessories*. People from all over the world have written to tell me how exciting it is to watch a kid's face light up in delight when they hand him or her a balloon replica of a favorite animal.

Now that I *have* a child, I'm even more aware of the thrill of pleasing youngsters with simple things. And one day it dawned on me that many kids had not only favorite animals but favorite characters—not just a mouse, for instance, but Mickey Mouse. (I must confess a weakness for certain characters myself.) So I went to work creating and perfecting some of the all-time classic cartoon and fictional favorites. I had a blast figuring out how to get Bullwinkle's hump just right, and finding the correct proportions for a Teenage Mutant Ninja Turtle. I hope you have as much fun making them.

Balloon Cartoons is designed to be rewarding for novice balloon sculptors as well as advanced balloonologists, so please don't fret if you haven't read any of my previous books. I've presented these balloon characters roughly in order of difficulty, so if this is your first experience twisting balloons, you might do best to start at the beginning of the book. First, there is important information on how to inflate, tie, and handle balloons in the beginning pages. More important, certain crucial points and phrases are explained in depth in the instructions for the first few animals, and if you start too far ahead, you might end up in one large, twisted balloon knot. After you've made the first two or three animals, let your confidence be your guide.

When you begin making each balloon character, I suggest that you read through all of the instructions for that character first. That way you'll have an idea of what to expect, and you won't end up with a Dumbo head on a Bugs Bunny body because, hands full of balloons, you turned to the wrong page!

This book comes with a starter supply of 20 balloons, but don't be disheartened if you're not a professional balloon sculptor by the time they run out. You'll get much better with a little practice, and, once you start making these and giving them to the children and older-than-children children in your life, you'll get a lot of practice! I suggest you try your local magic, novelty, or joke shop if you want to buy more of these balloons, but in case you can't find them anywhere I've included a few mail-order sources at the end of the book. Be sure to ask for the #260 variety of pencil balloons.

This book also comes with a pump, because pencil balloons are notoriously difficult to inflate. Even if your lungs are exceptionally strong and you can blow up the balloons yourself, you'll appreciate the pump after you've made a few animals!

If you *are* familiar with my other books, you'll notice a subtle but important difference in this one. With cartoon characters, small details, such as the tilt of a head or the angle of a tail, can make all the difference in conveying the personality of the animals. For that reason, you may have to play with the figures a bit to get everything just right, and the size of the uninflated tail end of your balloon is quite important. You may want to use a ruler to measure this tail when inflating your balloons. I've even improved my Snoopy, which originally appeared in *Balloon Animals*, to give it just the right "Snoopiness." With a little practice, you'll have no problem fashioning each character's distinguishing features with ease.

Balloons have an uncanny universal appeal, and with this new cartoon realm, I'm sure you'll be able to make many people, including yourself, practically pop with happiness!

BEFORE
YOU START

A FEW REMARKS ABOUT THE BALLOONS

Always keep your balloons in a cool, dry place, away from direct sunlight; both heat and sunlight make balloons more susceptible to popping. This will keep them fresh for at least a few months. I would also suggest taking a look at your fingernails to make sure that you have no sharp corners on any of them, which could also cause a balloon you are twisting to pop. Any jewelry, such as rings or bracelets, that could accidentally puncture a balloon should be removed before you begin twisting.

After you've inflated and tied a balloon (instructions for inflating and tying are in the next section) be sure to keep it away from any sharp objects. I suggest keeping it off the floor as well, as there are frequently tiny, sharp particles on the floor that can pop balloons. Avoid running your hands up and down the sides of the balloon. Though it makes an interesting sound (for some people), it can weaken the balloon and cause it to pop.

Always begin twisting your balloon from the end where it is tied and work toward the uninflated end. This will allow the air in the balloon to move downward as you make your twists. If you are ever in doubt as to how exactly to hold the balloon, please consult the photos that accompany each step. In fact, you may find it easier to make all the twists holding the balloon as shown, whether you are right- or left-handed; switching doesn't make it any easier and will make the photos more difficult to follow. If you find another method of twisting works best for you, by all means use it. Whatever gets the job done! Smaller bubbles, such as 1-inch or ½-inch bubbles, need a few extra twists to hold them in place.

Not all of these balloons are exactly the same size. While we have packaged the very best balloons available with this kit, some are a little shorter or longer than others. Because of this, some of your characters might end up looking slightly different from the ones in the photos. Remember, your balloon characters don't need to look exactly like mine to be wonderful. After you've made a few animals, you may feel that it is a better idea to keep the proportions right than to try to measure each bubble that you make. As I mentioned in the introduction, the most important measurement to make for each character is the amount of balloon that is left *uninflated* at the tail end when you first inflate your balloon. It may also help to know that these animals were designed to be flexible at the end. Feet can be a little smaller if you're running out of balloon, or larger if you have too much. At any rate, if you follow the pictures closely, you should end up with balloon characters that look remarkably similar to mine.

Remember that these balloons are made to be used for twisting. They are stronger than ordinary balloons, and for this reason you needn't be afraid to twist them, turn them, stretch them, or do anything that the instructions tell you to do to them. Occasionally, however, balloons do pop, through no fault of your own. Balloons are not perfect, and sometimes a balloon will have a weak spot due to a manufacturing imperfection. For this reason it is wise to avoid twisting balloons in any place where a sudden popping noise would be disruptive.

I don't advise drawing on these balloons, as it increases the chances that the balloons will pop. If you absolutely can't resist, please use a felt-tip marker.

Reminder: DON'T put inflated, tied balloons in your mouth.

INFLATING THE BALLOON

I recommend using the small hand pump included in this kit to blow up your balloons. Pencil balloons are difficult to inflate by mouth, and the pump works quite well. Using the pump will also allow you to make as many balloon animals as you want without getting tired from inflating them. Here are a few suggestions for inflating the balloons:

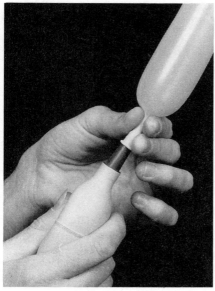

1. Stretch the balloon lengthwise a few times before you inflate it. Slip the end of the balloon over the nozzle of the pump. Roll the neck of the balloon about 1 inch over the nozzle. Hold it in place with the thumb and index finger of one hand. With your other hand, slowly begin inflating the balloon by squeezing and releasing the bulb of the pump.

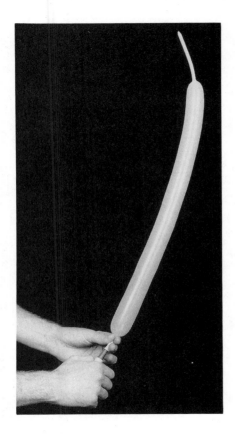

2. Fill the balloon until there is an appropriate length of tail on the end. Each animal requires a specific amount of tail, which allows the air in the balloon to expand as you make your twists. Don't worry if your balloon looks a bit curvier than the one shown—it won't matter once your balloon cartoon is twisted.

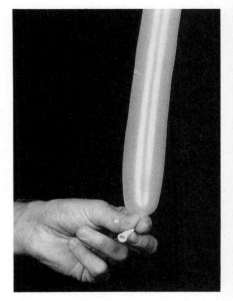

3. Slip the neck of the balloon off the nozzle of the pump, but continue pinching the neck of the balloon to keep the air inside.

TYING THE BALLOON

There are many good ways to tie a balloon. Any way that works for you is fine. These are the steps that I follow:

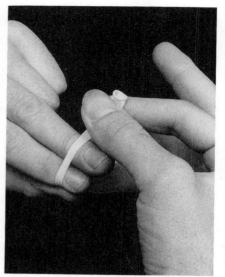

1. Let a tiny bit of air out of the balloon so that the neck of the balloon is a little longer and more flexible. Hold the neck of the balloon between your thumb and index finger.

2. Stretch the neck of the balloon over the backs of your index and middle fingers.

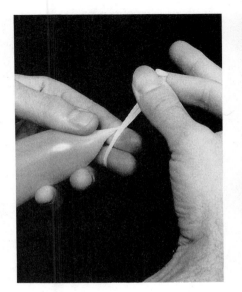 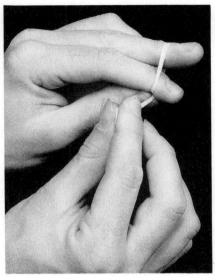 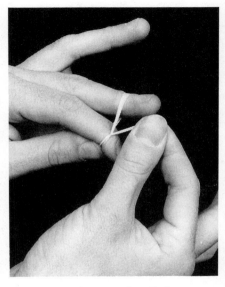

3. Continue stretching the neck of the balloon around the fronts of your index and middle fingers.

4. Separate your index and middle fingers to create a small space.

5. Push the neck of the balloon through this space.

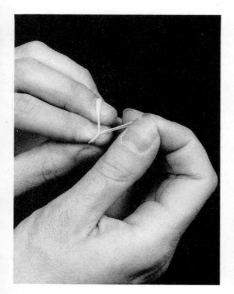

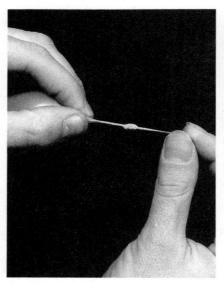

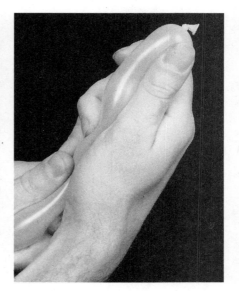

6. Holding the neck of the balloon, slide the rest of the balloon off your index and middle fingers.

7. Give a little tug and you have your knot.

8. IMPORTANT: Before you begin twisting any of the animals in this book, squeeze each balloon gently at the knot end to lessen the tension in the balloon.

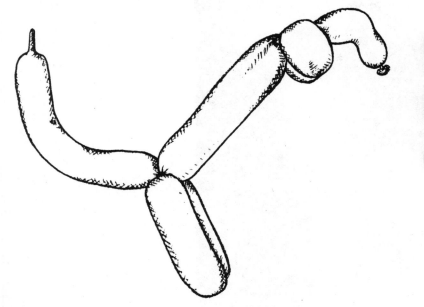

BEGINNER BALLOON CARTOONS

DINO THE DINOSAUR

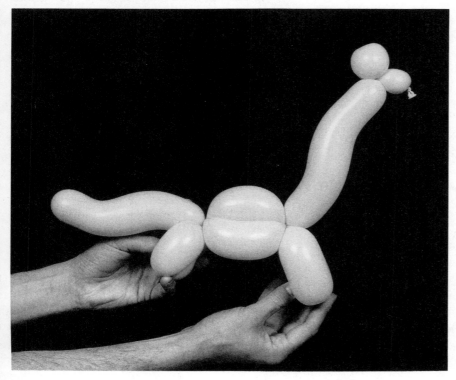

Man's best friend . . . in a
Stone Age family.

 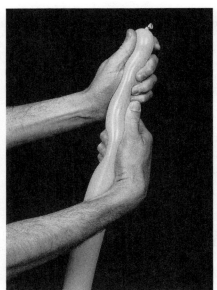 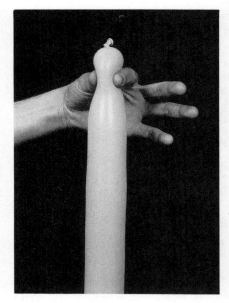

1. Inflate a balloon, leaving a 4-inch tail on the end, and tie a knot.

2. Squeeze the balloon well, just below the knot, to lessen the tension in the balloon.

3. Pinch the balloon one-half inch from the knot. Your pinch will create a tiny ½-inch bubble.

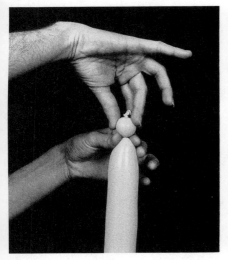

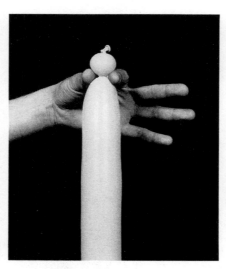

4. With your free hand, grasp the ½-inch bubble that is formed by your pinch and twist it around in a circle a few times. Smaller bubbles like this one need a few extra twists.

5. You'll have to hold on to this ½-inch bubble for a few moments; it won't stay in place by itself.

6. While you're holding on to the ½-inch bubble, pinch the balloon again, one-half inch below the first ½-inch bubble. This will create a second ½-inch bubble beneath the first. Try using one hand for this so your other hand will be free for the next step.

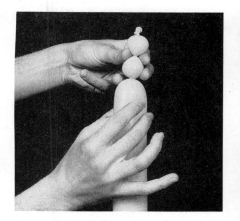

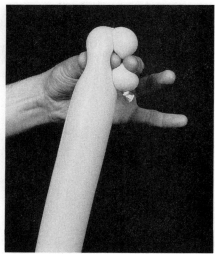

twist between the two ½-inch bubbles. You will notice that your pinch creates a third ½-inch bubble beside the second one.

7. Grasp the remaining length of balloon just below the pinch that forms your second ½-inch bubble. While continuing to hold on to your pinch, twist the remaining length of balloon around in a circle. This will create a second ½-inch bubble.

8. Fold both of these ½-inch bubbles down alongside the remaining length of balloon and pinch the remaining length of balloon at the point where it meets the

17

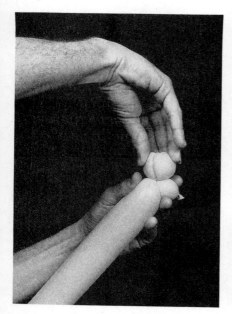

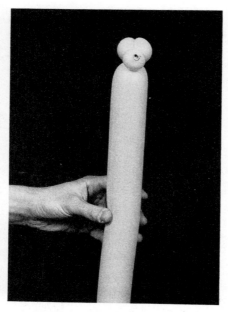

twists and forms Dino's head and ears. This last twist will be used frequently throughout the book and will be referred to as the *locking twist*. Now your hands are free to continue making Dino.

9. Take the second and third ½-inch bubbles and twist them, rotating them together, around in a circle.

10. Twist them around in a circle, about two full turns, until they stay in place. This rotating locks your previous

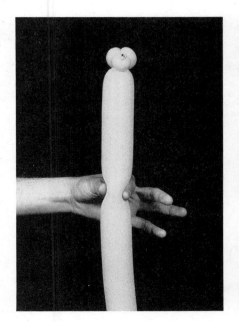 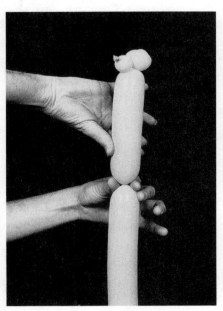 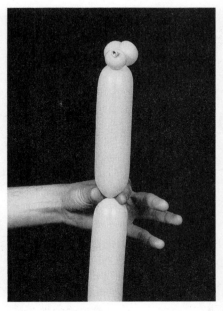

11. Pinch the balloon seven inches below the head of your Dino.

12. With your free hand, twist the 7-inch section of balloon around, two full turns. This twist forms Dino's neck.

13. Gently hold this twist with the thumb and index finger of one hand so that it doesn't untwist.

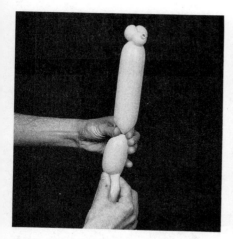

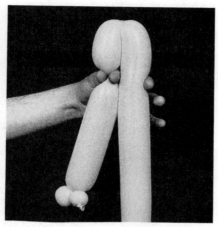

pinch will form another 3-inch bubble beside the first one.

14. Still holding on to that twist, pinch the balloon three inches below the 7-inch bubble and twist your hands in opposite directions at the pinch until the balloon twists again. This twist forms one of Dino's front legs.

15. Fold both of these bubbles down alongside the remaining length of balloon. Pinch the remaining length of balloon at the point where it meets the twist between the 7-inch bubble and the 3-inch bubble. Your

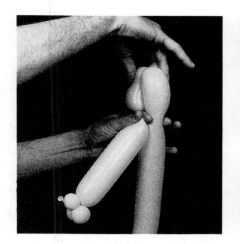

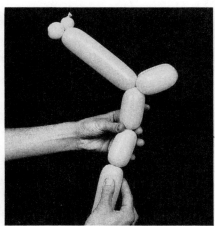

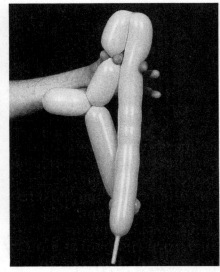

16. Twist both 3-inch bubbles, rotating them together, around in a circle a couple of times. This is your second locking twist, and it will hold your new bubbles in place.

17. Pinch off and twist two more 3-inch bubbles directly below the locking twist you just made. Hold on to them for a moment.

18. Fold both of the 3-inch bubbles down alongside the remaining length of balloon. Pinch the remaining length of balloon at the point where it meets the twist between the 3-inch bubbles. This pinch will create another 3-inch bubble beside the second one.

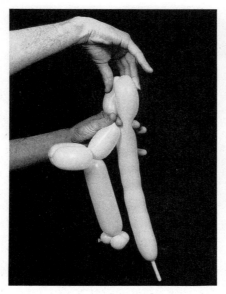

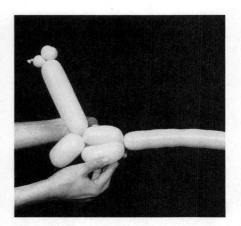

19. Twist the second and third 3-inch bubbles, rotating them together, around in a circle a couple of times. This is another locking twist.

20. Lay the first 3-inch bubble down on top of the second two 3-inch bubbles.

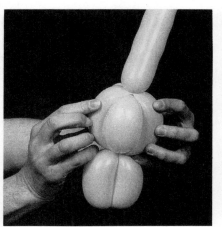

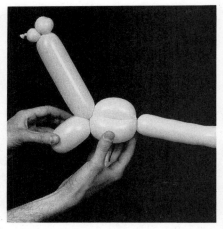

21. Gently roll the second two 3-inch bubbles around the first one.

22. Push the first 3-inch bubble through the second two 3-inch bubbles. Roll the second two 3-inch bubbles around the first one until the first 3-inch bubble is all the way through the second two.

23. Rotate all three 3-inch bubbles together until the first one lies on top of the second two, at Dino's back.

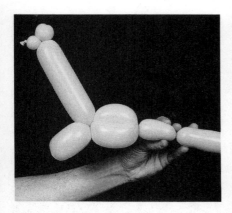

behind the cluster of 3-inch bubbles. Your pinch will form another 2-inch bubble beside the first one.

24. Squeeze the remaining length of balloon, directly behind the cluster of 3-inch bubbles, to extend the air in the balloon a little. Pinch off and twist a 2-inch bubble behind the cluster of 3-inch bubbles.

25. Fold the remaining length of balloon over so that it is adjacent to the 2-inch bubble. Pinch the remaining length of balloon where it meets the twist at the beginning of the 2-inch bubble, directly

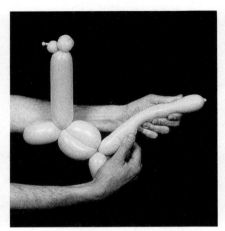

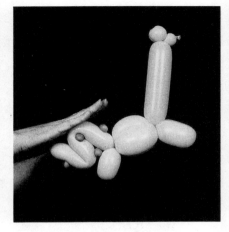

26. Twist the two 2-inch bubbles, rotating them together, around in a circle a couple of times until they are locked in place. This forms Dino's back legs.

27. Squeeze the remaining length of balloon until the air in it expands to fill its entire length and makes the remaining length softer and more pliable.

28. Fold the remaining length of balloon up into an S-shape. Rub the fold gently with your hand and breathe warm air from your mouth onto the folds to help the S keep its shape.

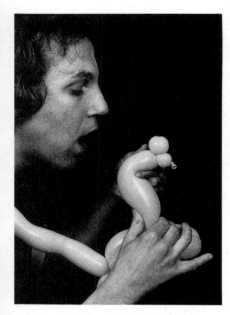

breathe warm air onto
the folds to help them
keep their shape.

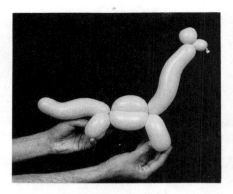

30. Twist and bend Dino's
S-shaped tail until you
get it to lie down
somewhat, and you
have finished Dino the
Dinosaur.

Congratulations! You've
completed your first
Balloon Cartoon!

29. Return to the 7-inch
bubble that is Dino's
neck and fold it up into
an S-shape as well.
Again, rub it and

THE ROADRUNNER

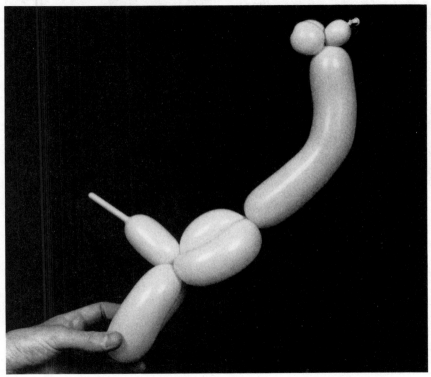

Beep, beep! This is the Roadrunner, posed while in motion, as he is often remembered.

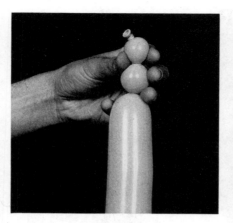

1. Inflate a balloon, leaving a 6-inch tail on the end, and tie a knot. Squeeze well, just below the knot, to lessen the tension in the balloon.

2. Pinch off and twist two tiny ½-inch bubbles, just as you did for Dino the Dinosaur. Make sure you twist each of these small bubbles around a couple of extra times to secure it. Hold on to both twists so that they don't untwist.

3. Fold both of the ½-inch bubbles down alongside the remaining length of balloon and pinch the remaining length of balloon where it meets the twist between the two ½-inch bubbles. This pinch will create a third ½-inch bubble.

28

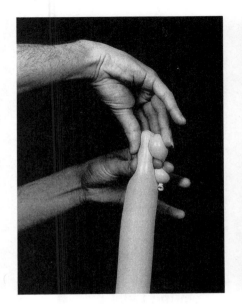

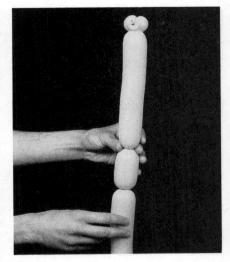

4. Twist the second and third ½-inch bubbles, rotating them together, around in a circle a couple of times. This is a locking twist.

5. You have just made the same head that you made for Dino the Dinosaur. This is what it looks like.

6. From the base of the Roadrunner's head, pinch off and twist an 8-inch bubble, followed by a 3-inch bubble. Hold on to both twists so that they don't untwist.

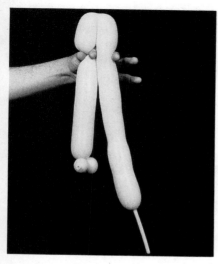

3-inch bubble. This pinch will form another 3-inch bubble beside the first one.

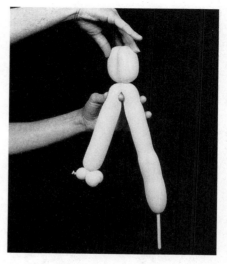

7. Fold both of these bubbles down alongside the remaining length of balloon. Pinch the remaining length of balloon where it meets the twist between the 8-inch bubble and the

8. Join the bubbles with a locking twist by twisting the two 3-inch bubbles, rotating them together, around in a circle a couple of times.

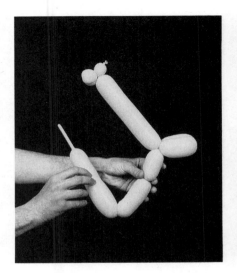

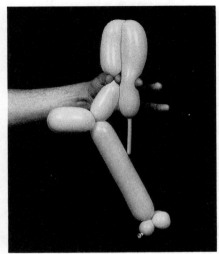

3-inch bubble. Your pinch will form another 3-inch bubble beside the first one. Make sure that a little bit of the inflated part of the balloon stays outside of your pinch. This last bit will be the tail of your Roadrunner.

9. From the point of your last locking twist, pinch off and twist a 2-inch bubble, followed by a 3-inch bubble. Hold on to both of these twists so that they don't untwist.

10. Fold both of these bubbles down alongside the remaining length of balloon. Pinch the remaining length of balloon where it meets the twist between the 2-inch bubble and the

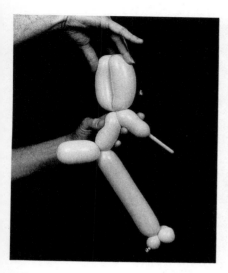

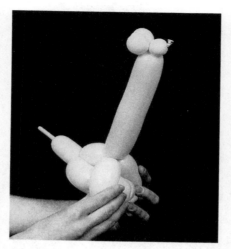

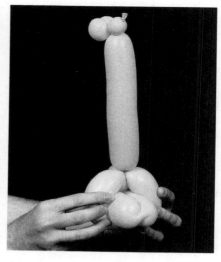

11. Join the bubbles with a locking twist.

12. Return to the first set of 3-inch bubbles that you made earlier. Gently spread them apart with your fingers and push the second set of 3-inch bubbles, end first, down between them.

13. Gently roll the first two 3-inch bubbles around the second two 3-inch bubbles.

32

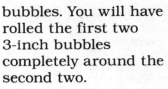

bubbles. You will have rolled the first two 3-inch bubbles completely around the second two.

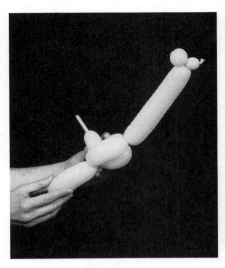

14. Continue rolling the first two 3-inch bubbles around the second two 3-inch bubbles until the first two 3-inch bubbles reach the twist at the back of the second two 3-inch

15. Now tuck the twist between the first two 3-inch bubbles down into the twist at the back of the second two 3-inch bubbles. Lift the little bubble at the very end of the balloon, which is the tail, and

wedge the twist between the first two 3-inch bubbles down under the tail. It may seem a little tricky, but if you are gentle it should fit in there nicely.

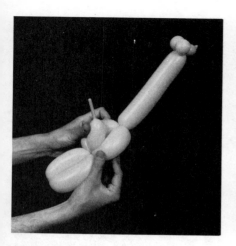

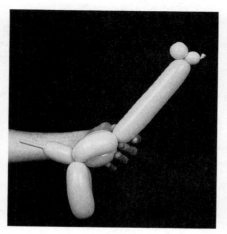

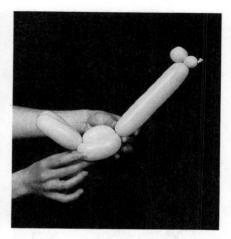

16. This is another picture of the tuck you just made.

17. This is what your Roadrunner looks like so far. The first two 3-inch bubbles are in the middle of your Roadrunner, while the second two 3-inch bubbles are on the bottom.

18. Rotate the first two 3-inch bubbles, which now adjoin the 2-inch bubble as well, around so that the 2-inch bubble is on top instead of on the bottom.

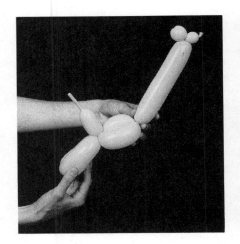

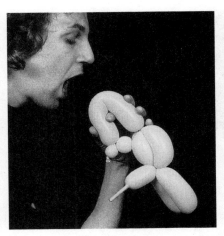

21. This is the completed Roadrunner.

19. If your Roadrunner's tail is aligned differently from the one shown in the photo, hold the second two 3-inch bubbles and the tail in one hand and rotate them together so that the tail is also on top.

20. Return to the 8-inch bubble that is the neck and bend it in half backward. Rub the fold gently with your hand. Breathe a little warm air onto the fold; this also helps to bend it slightly.

THE VERY HUNGRY CATERPILLAR

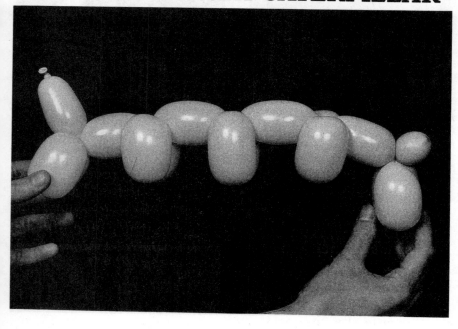

This popular character is simple to make and looks quite adorable.

  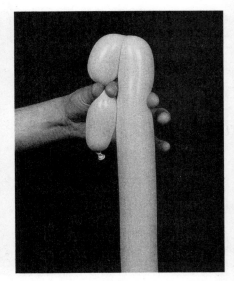

1. Inflate a balloon, leaving a 6-inch tail on the end, and tie a knot. Squeeze the balloon well, just below the knot, to lessen the tension in the balloon.

2. Pinch off and twist two 2-inch bubbles. Hold on to them so that they don't untwist.

3. Fold both of these bubbles down alongside the remaining length of balloon.

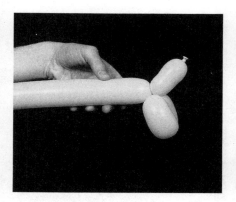

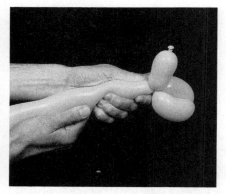

4. Join the bubbles with a locking twist.

5. This is what one section of your balloon looks like. You'll notice that this first section is the head and two legs of your Hungry Caterpillar. You will repeat these three steps *four* more times, exactly the same way, using only 2-inch bubbles.

6. Squeeze the balloon again, just below the head and legs, to lessen the tension in the remaining balloon. You will squeeze the balloon well after *each* locking twist.

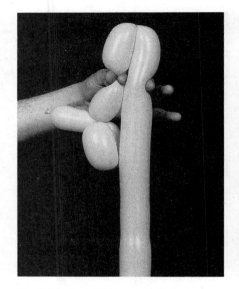

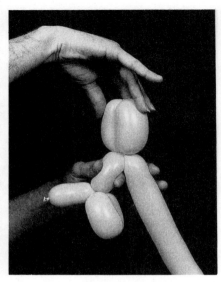

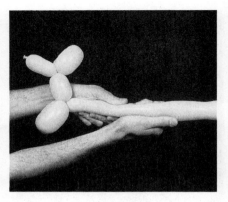

7. Pinch off and twist two more 2-inch bubbles and fold them down alongside the remaining length of balloon.

8. Join the bubbles with a locking twist.

9. Squeeze the balloon well, just below the last section of 2-inch bubbles that you made. Do you see the pattern?

twist and to leave a little balloon at the very end so that you can secure your last twist. This is what the balloon will look like when you have finished.

10. Continue this pattern of two 2-inch bubbles followed by a locking twist until you have run out of balloon. You should be able to do this a total of five times altogether. Remember to squeeze the balloon well after each locking

11. Make sure that all of the legs of your Caterpillar are pointing downward.

slightly, and take the first two body sections that you made. Wedge them down into the 2-inch bubbles that make up the first pair of legs. You will press them between the pair of legs until they stick there.

12. You will now wedge each of the body sections (these are the sections that connect the legs) into each of the legs sections. You will do this two body sections at a time. Ignore the head, which should point up

13. This is what your balloon will look like when you've done the first two.

14. Continue wedging the body sections, two at a time.

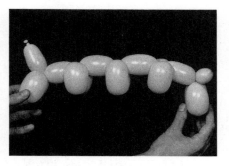

15. As you work your way down the body of the Hungry Caterpillar, wedging the body sections into the pairs of legs, one or two of the body sections may pop out. Simply replace them until you have all the body sections wedged between all the legs sections. This is the completed Very Hungry Caterpillar. You might be a little hungry yourself after all that work.

TYRANNOSAURUS REX

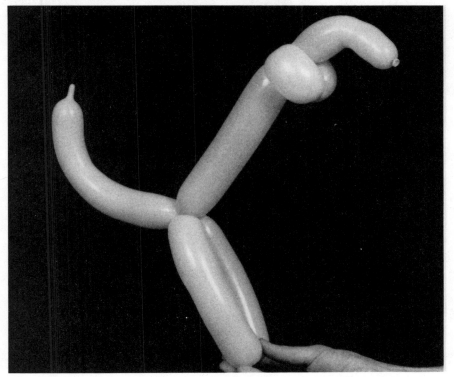

I just couldn't resist including the champion of all dinosaurs in this book. It's a perennial kids' favorite.

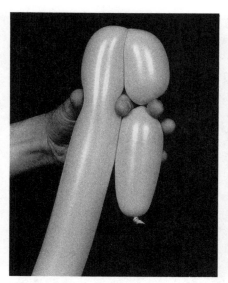

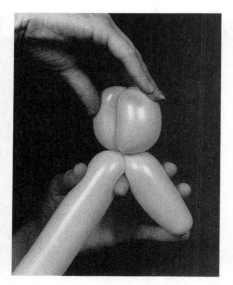

1. Inflate a balloon, leaving a 3-inch tail on the end, and tie a knot. Squeeze the balloon well, just below the knot, to lessen the tension in the balloon.

2. Make a 4-inch bubble, followed by a 2½-inch bubble, and fold both of these bubbles down alongside the remaining length of balloon.

3. Join the bubbles with a locking twist. This will create the head and the small forelegs of your Tyrannosaurus Rex.

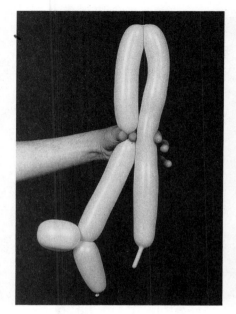

between the two 8-inch bubbles. This will create the body and long back legs of your Tyrannosaurus.

4. Make two 8-inch bubbles and fold both of them down alongside the remaining length of balloon.

5. Join the bubbles with a locking twist at the point where the remaining length of balloon meets the twist

45

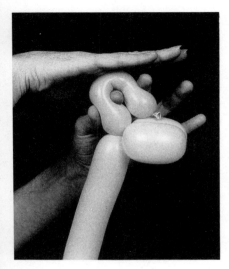

extra balloon at the tip. Fold the 4-inch bubble in half with one hand and gently rub the fold with your other hand. This will help bend the 4-inch bubble.

6. Return to the first 4-inch bubble that you made at the knot end of the balloon and give a gentle tug on the knot while squeezing the base of the bubble. This will release a little

7. Breathing warm air from your mouth on to the fold in the balloon will also help to bend it.

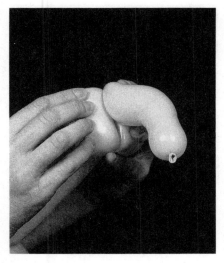

4-inch bubble through
the 2½-inch bubbles;
just wedge it in there.

8. Gently separate the two
2½-inch bubbles that
form the forelegs, and
wedge the bottom of
the 4-inch bubble that
forms the head down
into the 2½-inch
bubbles. Don't push the

9. Do the same thing with
the 8-inch bubble that
forms the body at the
point where it meets
the forelegs. Again,
wedge it in there, don't
push it through.

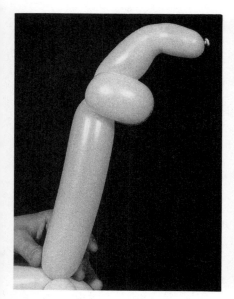

12. This is the Tyrannosaurus Rex.

10. This is what it will look like when you've done it correctly. It might take a couple of tries to get it right.

11. Return to the tail section and bend it in an arc until it is slightly curved. Rub the fold in the tail with your other hand.

RUDOLPH THE RED-NOSED REINDEER

This one's a real crowd
pleaser, especially around
the holidays.

knot, to lessen the tension in the balloon.

2. Make a 2-inch bubble, followed by four 1½-inch bubbles. Don't forget to give these small bubbles a couple of extra twists and to hold finished bubbles securely as you work on the next ones. Now fold all of these bubbles over so that the twist

after your last 1½-inch bubble meets the twist between the 2-inch bubble and the first 1½-inch bubble.

1. Inflate a balloon, leaving a 5-inch tail on the end, and tie a knot. Squeeze the balloon well, just below the

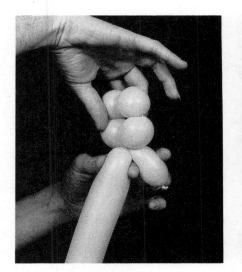 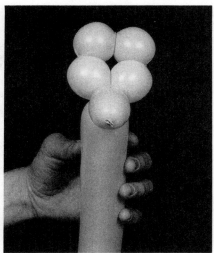 

3. Grasping all of the 1½-inch bubbles, rotate them around in a circle a couple of times at the point where those two twists meet.

4. This is what Rudolph looks like so far.

5. Make four more 1½-inch bubbles, and fold them over so that the twist after the last 1½-inch bubble meets the point where you have joined your other twists.

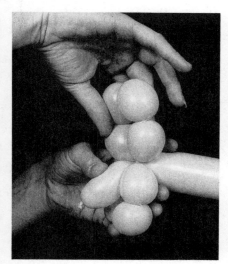  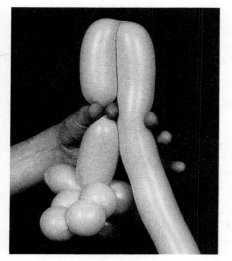

6. Holding all four of these 1½-inch bubbles, rotate them around in a circle a couple of times at the point where those two twists meet.

7. If necessary, arrange the antlers in the proper position, as shown. This is what Rudolph's head looks like.

8. Make a 3-inch bubble for the neck, followed by a 4-inch bubble for one of the front legs, and fold both of these bubbles down alongside the remaining length of balloon.

sure to leave a little
bubble on the very end
for the tail.

9. Join the bubbles with a
locking twist.

10. Make a 3-inch bubble
for the body, followed
by a 4-inch bubble for
one of the back legs,
and fold both of these
bubbles down alongside
the small remaining
length of balloon. Be

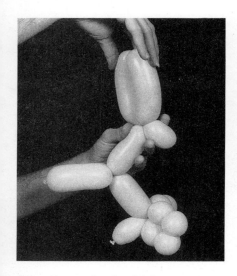

12. This is Rudolph the
Red-Nosed Reindeer.

11. Join the bubbles with a
locking twist.

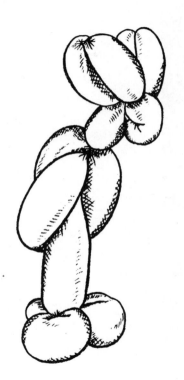

INTERMEDIATE
BALLOON
CARTOONS

SNOOPY

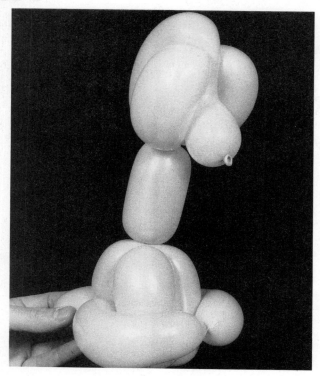

Now the world's most popular beagle can live at your house!

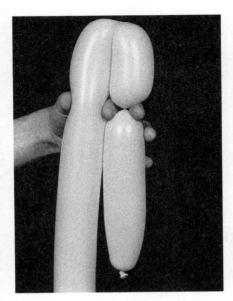

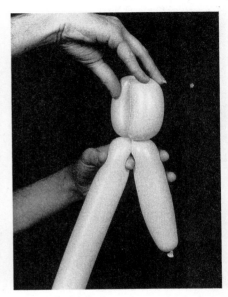

1. Inflate a balloon, leaving a 4-inch tail on the end, and tie a knot. Squeeze the balloon well, below the knot.

2. Make a 6-inch bubble and a 3-inch bubble, and fold both of these bubbles down alongside the remaining length of balloon.

3. Join the bubbles with a locking twist.

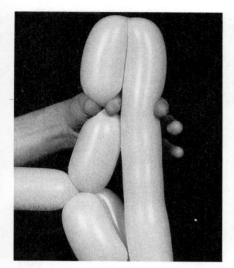

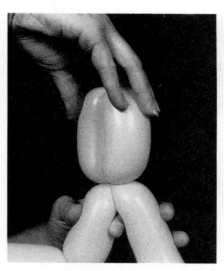

4. Make a 3-inch bubble for the neck, followed by a 3-inch bubble for one of the front legs, and fold both of these bubbles down alongside the remaining length of balloon.

5. Join the bubbles with a locking twist.

6. Make a 2-inch bubble for the body, followed by a 4-inch bubble for one of the back legs, and fold both of these bubbles down alongside the small remaining length of balloon. Be sure to leave a small bubble on the very end for the tail.

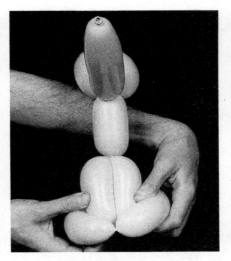

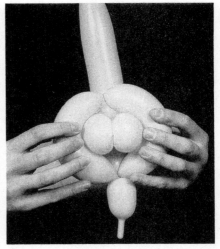

7. Join the bubbles with a locking twist.

8. Gently separate the two 4-inch bubbles that form the back legs of your Snoopy and insert the two 3-inch bubbles that form the front legs down between the two 4-inch bubbles.

9. Gently push the two 3-inch bubbles into the two 4-inch bubbles until the 3-inch bubbles are firmly in place. Your Snoopy should be able to sit securely, without falling over.

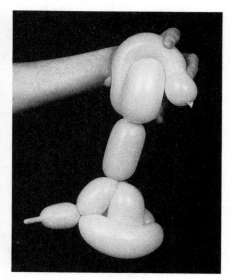

and bend it over the two 3-inch bubbles that form Snoopy's ears. This will help stretch the bubble for the next step.

10. This is what Snoopy looks like so far.

11. Position Snoopy so that the very first bubble you made—the 6-inch one—is pointing behind him. Take this 6-inch bubble, which will be Snoopy's nose,

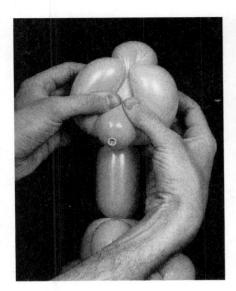

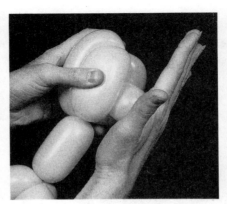

12. Gently spread the two 3-inch bubbles apart and push the 6-inch bubble between them firmly, at a downward angle, as shown.

13. Once the 6-inch bubble is firmly in place, gently squeeze the two 3-inch bubbles from the outside while gently pushing up on the tip of the 6-inch bubble with your other hand. This will give Snoopy's nose a slightly upturned look.

14. You might need to turn Snoopy's head around so that it faces forward. This is your completed Snoopy.

BUGS BUNNY

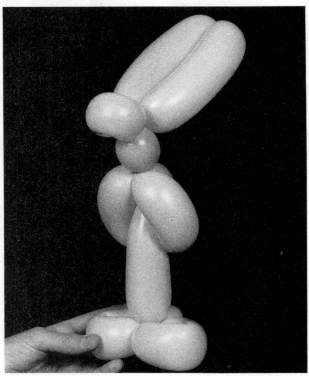

An irrepressible wabbit, and the original cartoon carrot nosher, in balloon form.

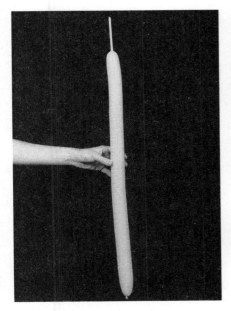

1. Inflate a balloon, leaving a 4-inch tail on the end, and tie a knot. Squeeze the balloon well, below the knot.

2. Make a 3-inch bubble, followed by a 6-inch bubble, and fold both of these bubbles down alongside the remaining length of balloon.

3. Join the bubbles with a locking twist.

63

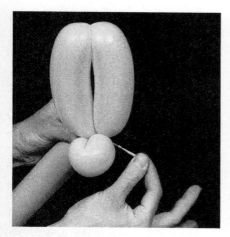

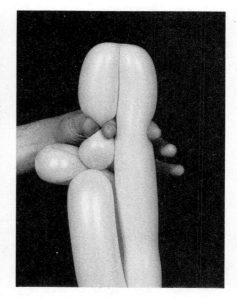

4. Fold the 3-inch bubble in half sideways, and pull the knot end around to the twist underneath the 6-inch ears. Wrap the knot around this twist a couple of times so the folded bubble holds its shape.

5. This is what Bugs looks like at this point.

6. Make a 1-inch bubble and a 3-inch bubble and fold both of these bubbles alongside the remaining length of balloon.

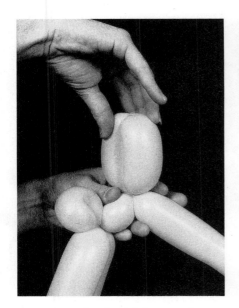 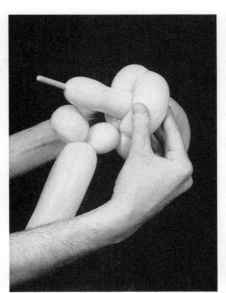 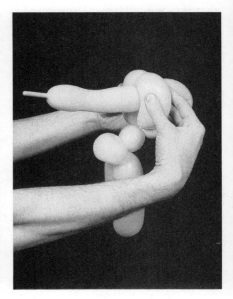

7. Join the bubbles with a locking twist.

8. Gently separate the two adjoining 3-inch bubbles and insert the remaining length of balloon, end first, between them.

9. Keep the 3-inch bubbles separated while pushing the remaining length of balloon through the 3-inch bubbles.

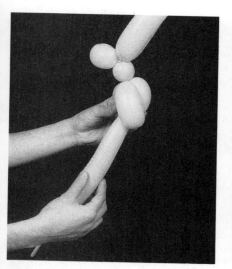

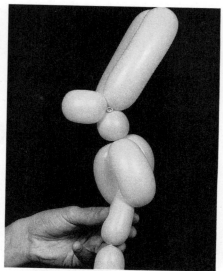

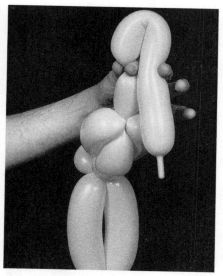

10. Pull the remaining length of balloon almost all the way through the 3-inch bubbles. Bend the remaining length of balloon so that it points straight down.

11. Make a twist in the remaining length of balloon, about three inches from where it exits the 3-inch bubbles, for Bugs's body.

12. From this last twist, pinch a 4-inch bubble and fold it in half so that the pinch you are holding meets the twist at the end of the body section.

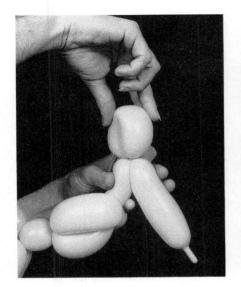

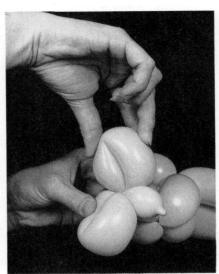

13. Turn this folded 4-inch bubble around in a circle a couple of times until it locks in place.

14. Repeat these last two steps with another folded 4-inch bubble. Be sure to leave a little bubble at the very end for Bugs's tail.

15. These folded 4-inch bubbles form Bugs's big feet.

 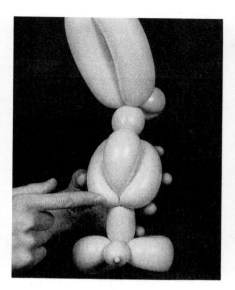 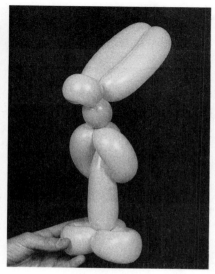

16. Return to the long bubble in the center of your character, which is Bugs's torso, and gently bend it backward almost in half so that Bugs will stand up straighter.

17. Position the two 3-inch bubbles, which are Bugs's arms, so that the twist between them is at Bugs's back.

18. This is Bugs Bunny.

MR. ED

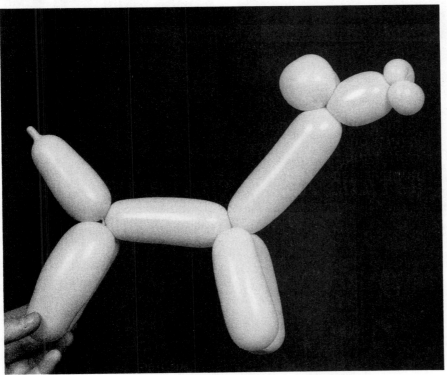

A horse, of course. If *your* Mr. Ed can talk, you might want to keep the fact to yourself.

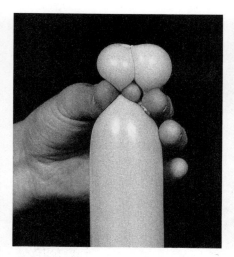

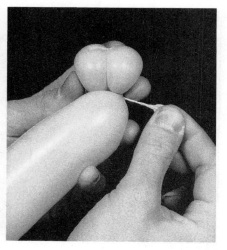

1. Inflate a balloon, leaving a 5-inch tail on the end, and tie a knot. Squeeze the balloon well, below the knot.

2. Make two tiny ½-inch bubbles and hold them down alongside *one another*.

3. Wrap the knot around the twist that follows the second ½-inch bubble. Be sure to wrap it around a few times so that it stays in place.

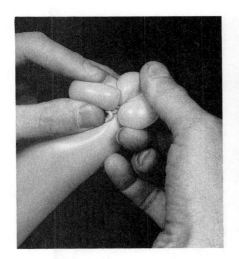

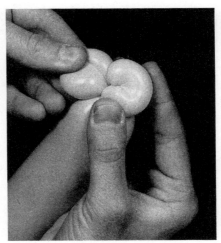

4. Hold on to one ½-inch bubble while you pinch the other one and twist it around in a circle a couple of times.

5. Pinch the other ½-inch bubble and twist it the same way. You have now made Mr. Ed's lips.

6. This is what Mr. Ed's mouth looks like at this point.

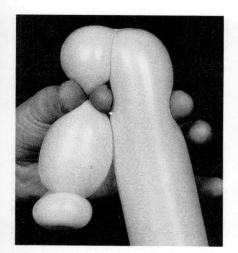

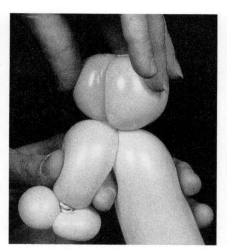

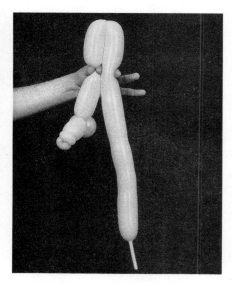

7. Make a 2-inch bubble for the muzzle, followed by a 1-inch bubble for one of the ears, and fold both of these bubbles down alongside the remaining length of balloon.

8. Join the bubbles with a locking twist.

9. Make a 4-inch bubble for the neck, followed by a 4-inch bubble for one of the front legs, and fold both of these bubbles down alongside the remaining length of balloon.

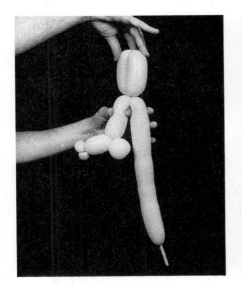

10. Join the bubbles with a locking twist.

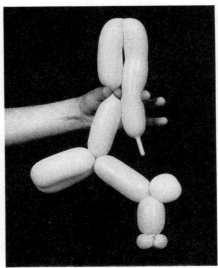

11. Make two more 4-inch bubbles and fold both of them down alongside the remaining length of balloon. Be sure to leave a little bubble on the end for a tail.

12. Join the bubbles with a locking twist.

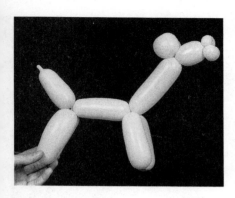

13. This is Mr. Ed.

DUMBO THE ELEPHANT

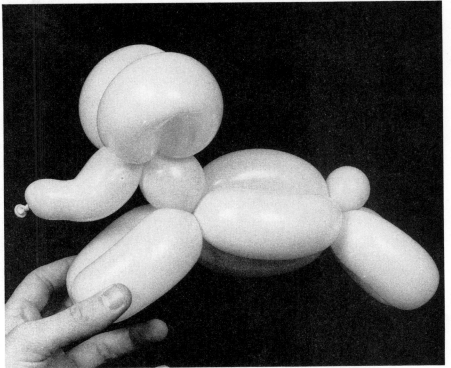

A lot of my friends say *Dumbo* was the first movie they ever saw. This pudgy pachyderm holds a special place in the hearts of kids of all ages.

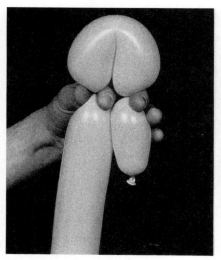

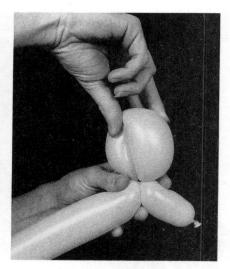

1. Inflate a balloon until you have a 4-inch tail on the end, and tie a knot. Squeeze the balloon well, below the knot.

2. Make a 2-inch bubble for the trunk, then pinch a 5-inch bubble and fold it in half so that the end of the 5-inch bubble meets the twist after the 2-inch bubble.

3. Rotate the folded 5-inch bubble around in a circle a couple of times so that it is locked in place. This creates one of Dumbo's floppy ears.

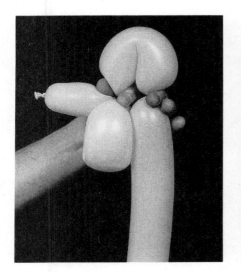 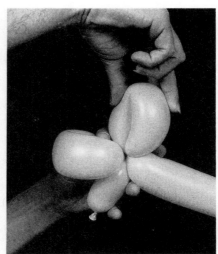 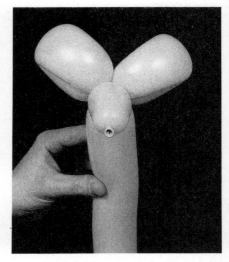

4. Do the same thing with another 5-inch bubble and join it at the same point.

5. Rotate this folded 5-inch bubble around in a circle, the same as in Step 3. Rotate it a couple of times so that it too is locked in place. This will create Dumbo's other ear.

6. This is what Dumbo's head looks like so far.

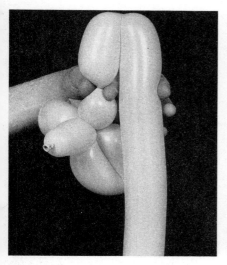 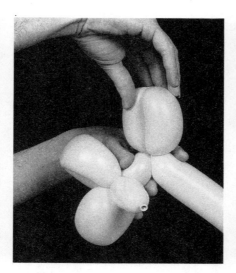 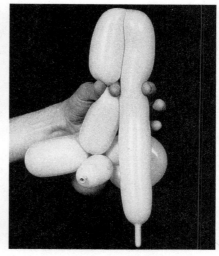

7. Make a 1-inch bubble for the neck and a 3-inch bubble for one of the front legs, and fold both of these bubbles down alongside the remaining length of balloon.

8. Join the bubbles with a locking twist. This creates the neck and both of Dumbo's front legs.

9. Make two 3-inch bubbles and fold both of them down alongside the remaining length of balloon.

10. Join the bubbles with a locking twist.

11. Lay the first 3-inch bubble down between the second two 3-inch bubbles.

12. Gently roll the second two 3-inch bubbles around the first 3-inch bubble.

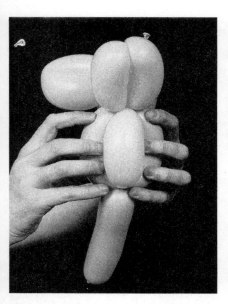

remaining length of balloon. If you find you are running out of balloon, it helps to squeeze the remaining length of balloon to extend the air in it just a little bit. Fold the 3-inch bubble down alongside the length that's left. Be sure to pinch off a little bubble at the very end for a tail.

13. Push the first 3-inch bubble all the way through the separated 3-inch bubbles.

14. If the first 3-inch bubble is not at Dumbo's back, twist his body around until it is. Make a 3-inch bubble with the

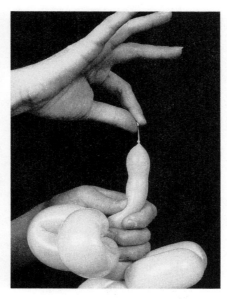

squeezing the base of
the 2-inch bubble at
the same time. This
releases a little extra
balloon in the bubble.

15. Twist the two 3-inch
bubbles around in a
circle a couple of times
until they are locked in
place.

16. Return to the 2-inch
bubble at the knot end
of the balloon, which is
the trunk of your
Dumbo. Gently tug on
the knot while

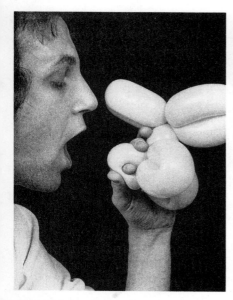

18. Turn the trunk so that it curves upward, and you have finished making Dumbo the Elephant.

17. Then fold the 2-inch bubble in half and breathe a little warm air on the fold to bend the 2-inch bubble.

GARFIELD

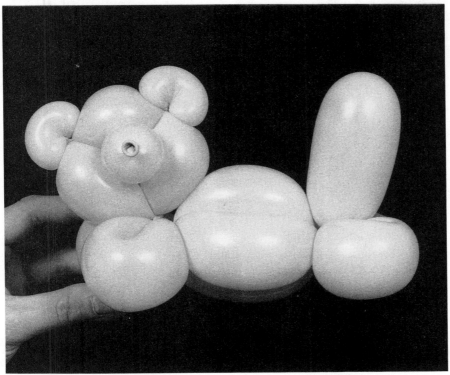

You can almost see the mischievousness in this chubby balloon cat. Keep your food hidden!

last 1½-inch bubble, and fold all of these bubbles over in a loop so that the twist after your first 1½-inch bubble meets the twist after your last 1½-inch bubble.

1. Inflate a balloon, leaving a 6-inch tail on the end, and tie a knot. Squeeze the balloon well, below the knot.

2. Make two 1½-inch bubbles, followed by a tiny ½-inch bubble, a 1-inch bubble, another ½-inch bubble, and one

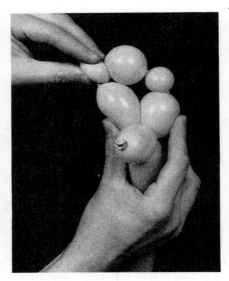

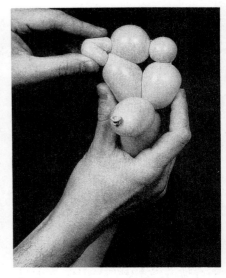

3. Hold the entire loop of bubbles and rotate it around in a circle a couple of times as shown, so that the bubbles are locked in place.

4. Pinch one of the tiny ½-inch bubbles and pull it out slightly from the loop of bubbles.

5. Twist it around on its ends a couple of times.

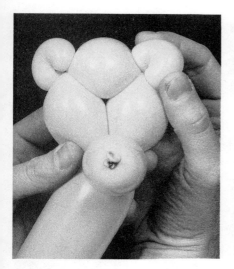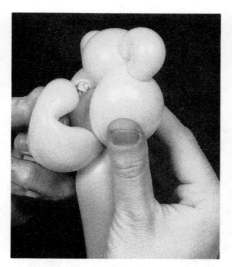

6. Do the same thing with the other ½-inch bubble. These are Garfield's ears.

7. Take the first 1½-inch bubble at the knot end and push the knot end back between the loop of bubbles.

8. Gently roll the loop of bubbles around the 1½-inch bubble until just a little of the knot end is sticking out through the loop.

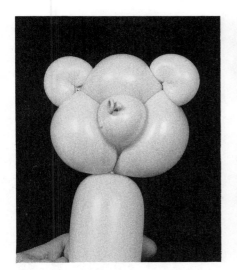

9. This is what Garfield's head looks like.

10. Directly beneath the head, pinch a 4-inch bubble and fold it in half so that the pinch you are holding meets the twist at the beginning of the 4-inch bubble.

11. Rotate the 4-inch bubble around in a circle so that it locks in place.

12. Do the same thing with another 4-inch bubble, and join it at the same point. These two 4-inch bubbles form Garfield's two front paws.

13. Make two 2½-inch bubbles and fold them down alongside the remaining length of balloon.

14. Join the bubbles with a locking twist.

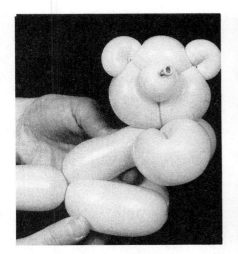

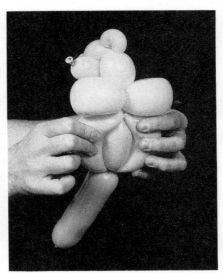

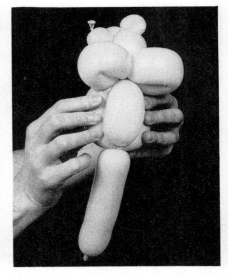

15. Lay the first 2½-inch bubble down between the second two 2½-inch bubbles.

16. Gently roll the second two 2½-inch bubbles up and around the first 2½-inch bubble.

17. Push the first 2½-inch bubble through the second two 2½-inch bubbles until the first 2½-inch bubble is all the way through the second two.

18. If you need to, rotate all three 2½-inch bubbles so that the first one, which you just pushed through the second two, is on top. Squeeze the remaining length of balloon to extend it a bit.

19. Pinch a 3-inch bubble and fold it in half.

20. Rotate the 3-inch bubble around in a circle so that it stays in place. This is one of Garfield's back paws.

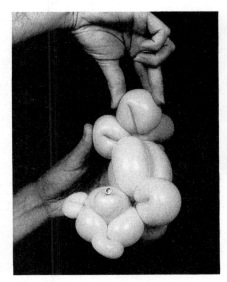

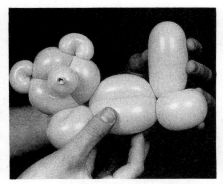

21. Repeat this with one more 3-inch bubble for the other back paw.

22. The remaining length of balloon, which will vary from balloon to balloon, will be used for the tail. You may need to squeeze the tail to fill it evenly with air. Make sure that it points straight up.

23. Position Garfield's head so that it rests comfortably on his front paws, and you have completed Garfield.

BULLWINKLE

I'd bet my pump that this great balloon cartoon would fool even Rocky!

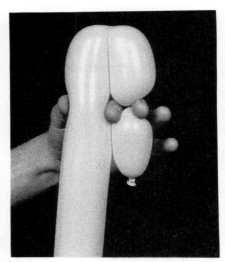

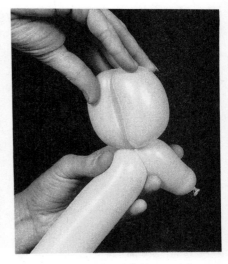

1. Inflate a balloon until you have a 5-inch tail on the end, and tie a knot. Squeeze the balloon well, below the knot.

2. Make a 2-inch bubble and a 2½-inch bubble and fold both of these bubbles down alongside the remaining length of balloon.

3. Join the bubbles with a locking twist.

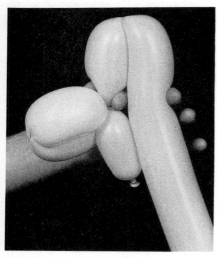

beginning of the 2½-inch bubble. This will form another 2½-inch bubble next to the first.

4. Make another 2½-inch bubble and fold it down alongside the remaining length of balloon. Pinch the remaining length of balloon where it meets the twist at the

5. Twist the two 2½-inch bubbles around in a circle a couple of times until they are locked in place. You have just completed Bullwinkle's antlers.

knot end, pulling the knot of the balloon back to the twist at the base of the 2-inch bubble, as shown.

6. Go back to the knot end of your balloon and give a gentle tug on the knot while squeezing the base of your 2-inch bubble. Fold the 2-inch bubble down one third of the way from the

7. Wrap the knot around the twist underneath both antlers. Wrap it around a couple of times so that it will stay in place. This bent 2-inch bubble is Bullwinkle's face.

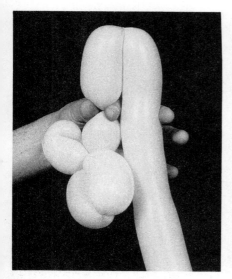

8. Make a 1½-inch bubble followed by a 3-inch bubble, and fold both of these bubbles down alongside the remaining length of balloon.

9. Join the bubbles with a locking twist.

10. Separate the two 3-inch bubbles that you have just made, and push the remaining length of balloon, end first, through the two separated 3-inch bubbles.

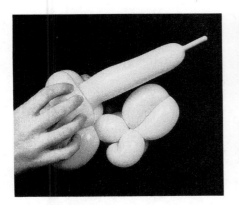

11. Keep the two 3-inch bubbles around the remaining length of balloon separated as you continue to push the remaining length through.

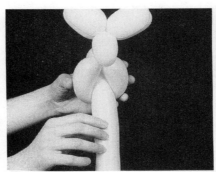

12. Push the remaining length almost all the way through the two separated 3-inch bubbles, and turn the balloon so that the two 3-inch bubbles, which are Bullwinkle's arms, are positioned as shown. Bend the remaining length of balloon so that it points straight down.

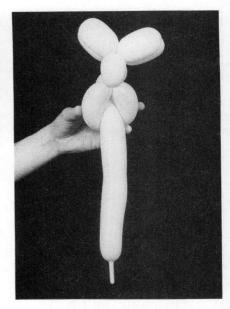

13. This is what Bullwinkle looks like so far.

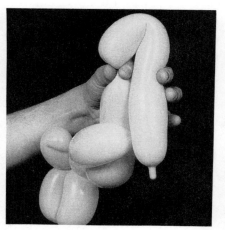

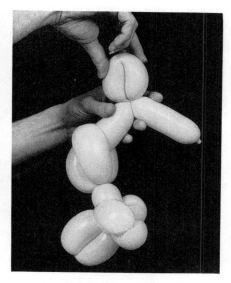

14. Make a bubble in the remaining length of balloon about two inches below where it emerges from Bullwinkle's arms. This forms Bullwinkle's body.

15. Squeeze the remaining length of balloon to extend it a little, and pinch a 3-inch section of the remaining length. Fold it in half so that the pinch you are holding meets the twist at the end of the body section.

16. Rotate the 3-inch bubble around in a circle a couple of times so that it is locked into place.

98

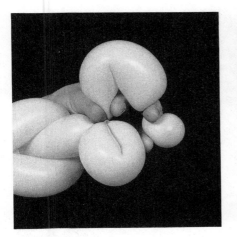

17. Make another 3-inch bubble with the remaining length of balloon. Be sure to leave a little bubble at the very end for a tail. Fold this 3-inch bubble in half, as you just did with the last 3-inch bubble.

18. Rotate this 3-inch bubble around in a circle until it locks into place.

19. Arrange these last two folded bubbles as shown in the photo. They are Bullwinkle's big feet.

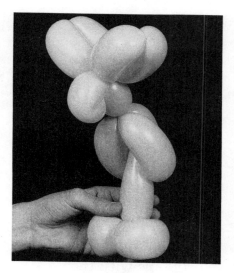

a little to straighten it, and your Bullwinkle will stand upright.

21. This is Bullwinkle.

20. Bend the long bubble in the middle of your Bullwinkle, which is his torso, backward. Rock it back and forth

TEENAGE MUTANT NINJA TURTLE

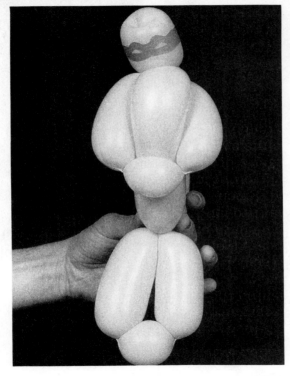

Cowabunga! I'm very proud of this creation. Of course, it's impossible to make the mask for the turtle using just a balloon, so I've provided a design and instructions for making a paper mask to affix to your new balloon hero.

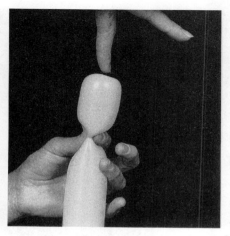

1. Inflate a balloon, leaving a 6-inch tail on the end, and tie a knot. Squeeze the balloon well, below the knot.

2. Push the knot back into the balloon about one and one-half inches and grab the knot, through the balloon, with your other hand.

3. Slowly remove your finger while still holding the knot with your other hand.

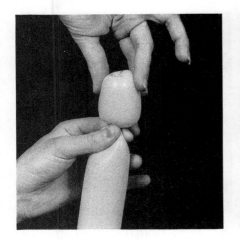

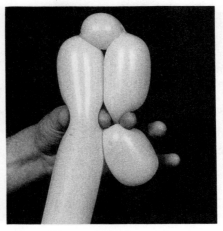

where it meets the twist at the beginning of your 3-inch bubble. Your pinch will form another 3-inch bubble beside the first one.

4. Twist the balloon around just *above* the knot a couple of times, forming a 1½-inch bubble. This will be the head of your turtle.

5. Now make a 3-inch bubble and a 1-inch bubble. Be sure to give a couple of extra twists on both sides of the 1-inch bubble. Fold the remaining length of balloon over and pinch the remaining length

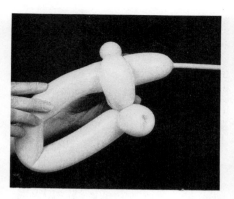

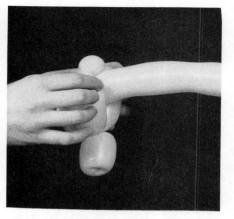

6. Rotate this series of bubbles around in a circle a couple of times until it is locked in place.

7. Gently spread apart the circle of balloons that you have just formed and insert the remaining length of balloon, end first, through the circle.

8. Keep holding the circle of bubbles apart and push the length of balloon through the circle of bubbles at the same time, until the length of balloon is *almost* all the way through the circle. You have just formed the chest of your turtle.

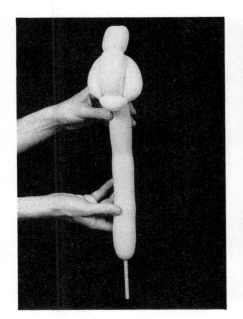 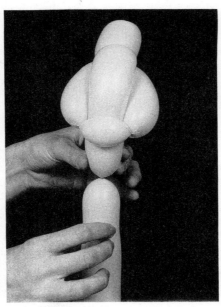 

9. Straighten the remaining length of balloon so that it points downward.

10. Make a twist in the remaining length about two inches from where it exits the circle of balloons.

11. Holding the twist you just made, make a 3-inch bubble and a 1-inch bubble, and fold them down alongside the remaining length of balloon. Pinch the remaining length of balloon where it meets the twist at the beginning of the 3-inch bubble. Again, your pinch will form an adjoining 3-inch bubble.

12. Twist this series of bubbles, rotating them together, around in a circle a couple of times until it is locked in place.

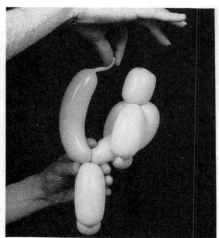

13. Take the tail end of the balloon and stretch the remaining length of balloon up to the head of your turtle.

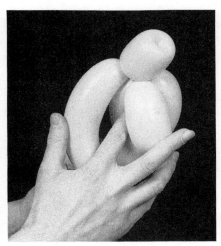

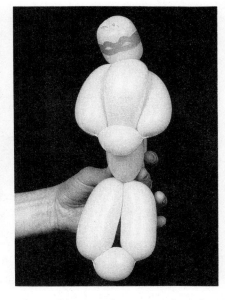

14. Wrap the uninflated tail of the balloon around the twist below your turtle's head.

15. Tuck the tail inside the body of your turtle so that it cannot be seen.

16. This is the completed Teenage Mutant Ninja Turtle.
(See the next page for the mask pattern and instructions.)

Trace the mask provided on
this page using a thin piece
of paper, and cut it out
carefully with a pair of
scissors. After you've cut it
out, you may want to color it
with a crayon to match your
favorite Ninja Turtle's mask
color. Wrap it around the
head of your turtle and tape
it on with a piece of
transparent tape.

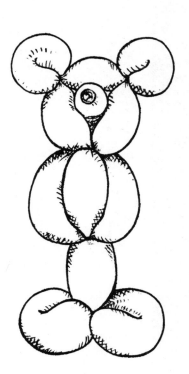

ADVANCED
BALLOON
CARTOONS

MICKEY MOUSE

Mickey's head is a challenge, but the finished animal is spectacular. You'll get a lot of requests for this much-adored mouse!

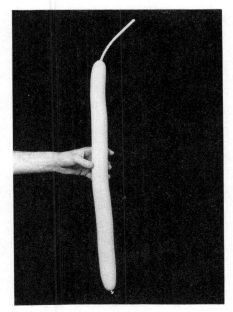

knot. It is important, as well, to squeeze the balloon after all but the last twist *in the next step only,* just below each twist.

1. Inflate a balloon, leaving a 6-inch tail on the end, and tie a knot. Squeeze the balloon *very* well, below the

2. Make a 2-inch bubble (and squeeze the balloon below the twist), followed by a 1½-inch bubble (squeeze), another 2-inch bubble (squeeze), another 1½-inch bubble (squeeze), yet another 2-inch bubble (squeeze), and one last 1½-inch bubble (no squeeze). Fold all of

these bubbles over in a loop so that the twist after the first bubble meets the twist after the last bubble.

  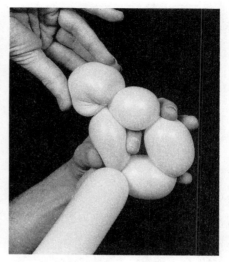

3. Hold the entire loop of bubbles and rotate it together around in a circle a couple of times as shown. This will lock them all in place.

4. Pinch the second 2-inch bubble and pull it out a little from the loop.

5. Twist this 2-inch bubble around on its ends a couple of times. This will feel a little tight, but it's not that difficult.

  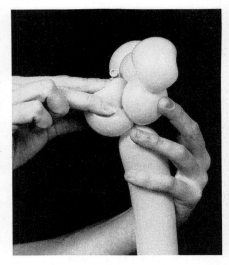

6. You have just formed one of Mickey's ears. This is what that ear looks like.

7. Do the same thing for the third 2-inch bubble to form Mickey's other ear. This is what both ears will look like when you are done.

8. Take the first 2-inch bubble you made and point the knot end back toward the loop of bubbles.

9. Gently roll the loop of
bubbles back over the
first 2-inch bubble.
This will feel a little
tight, but if you do it
gently it will work.

10. Roll the loop around
the first 2-inch bubble
until about half of the
2-inch bubble is
sticking out on each
side of the loop.

11. This is what Mickey
Mouse's head looks
like.

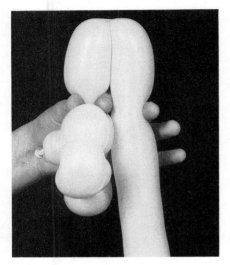

the twist at the beginning of the 3-inch bubble. This creates a second 3-inch bubble.

12. Make a 3-inch bubble for one of the arms, and fold this 3-inch bubble down alongside the remaining length of balloon. Pinch the remaining length of balloon where it meets

13. Join the bubbles with a locking twist at this point.

115

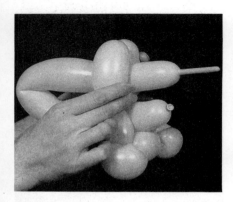

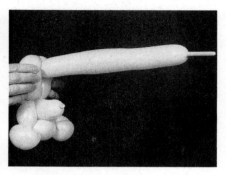

14. Gently spread the two 3-inch bubbles apart with your fingers and begin to push the remaining length of balloon, end first, through the separated 3-inch bubbles.

15. Keep the 3-inch bubbles separated while pushing the remaining length through them. Do this until almost all of the remaining length of balloon is through the separated 3-inch bubbles. If you need to, turn Mickey's head so that it points away from the remaining length of balloon. You have now completed Mickey's chest. Straighten the remaining length of balloon so that it points downward.

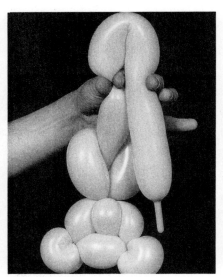

16. Make a twist in the remaining length of balloon, about two inches below where it exits the separated 3-inch bubbles, for Mickey's body.

17. From this last twist, pinch a 4-inch bubble and fold it in half so that the pinch you are holding meets the twist at the end of the body section.

18. Grasp the entire folded 4-inch bubble in one hand and twist it around in a circle a couple of times. This will lock it in place.

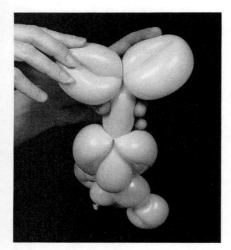

length before you make this last twist.

19. Repeat this with another folded 4-inch bubble, leaving a little bubble on the end of the balloon for a tail. If you need to, you can squeeze the remaining length of balloon to give it a little extra

20. Bend the long length of balloon that forms Mickey's torso backward and gently rock it back and forth so that the torso is straightened and Mickey will stand upright.

21. If you need to, position the two 3-inch bubbles that form Mickey's arms so that the twist between them is in front of Mickey's body as he faces forward.

22. This is the completed Mickey Mouse.

CURIOUS GEORGE

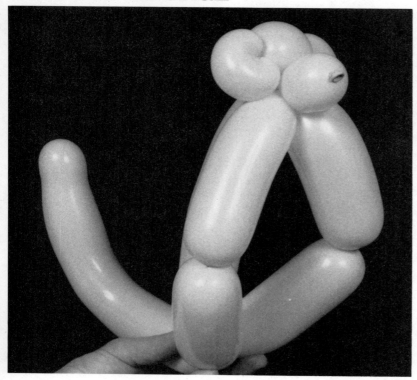

Like George himself, this animal is a bit tricky, but if you proceed slowly you shouldn't have any problems.

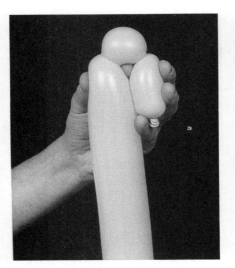

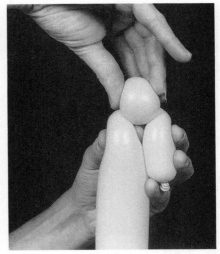

1. Inflate a balloon, leaving a 3-inch tail on the end, and tie a knot. Squeeze the balloon *very* well, below the knot.

2. Make a 1½-inch bubble, followed by a 1-inch bubble, and fold these two bubbles over so that the 1-inch bubble is sticking up.

3. Grab the 1-inch bubble with your free hand and pull it away from the rest of the balloon a little.

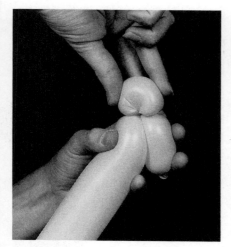

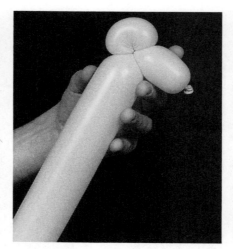

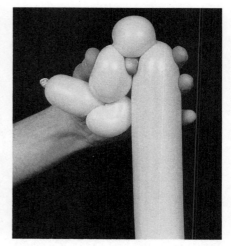

4. Twist the 1-inch bubble around on its ends a couple of times. This will lock it in place.

5. This is what your balloon looks like so far.

6. Make another 1½-inch bubble, followed by another 1-inch bubble, and fold these two bubbles over the same way that you did the last two, with the 1-inch bubble sticking up.

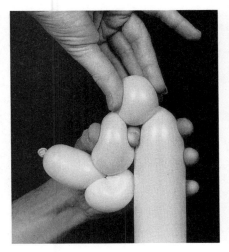 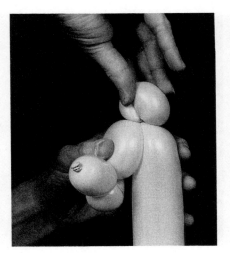 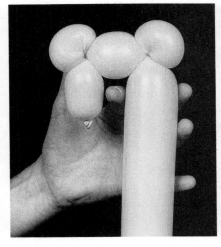

7. Pinch the 1-inch bubble and pull it away from the adjoining bubbles.

8. Twist it around on its ends the same way that you did with the last 1-inch bubble.

9. This is what you have so far.

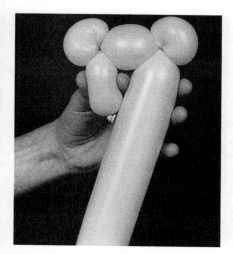

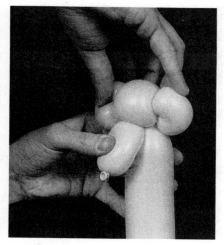

strong and should endure this easily. Twist them around a couple of times so that they stay in place.

10. Now fold the 1½-inch bubble at the knot end down alongside the remaining length of balloon.

11. Grasp all three of the other bubbles with your other hand and, holding them together, twist *all three* of them around in a circle. This will feel weird the first time you do it, but the balloons are very

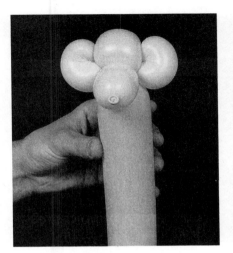

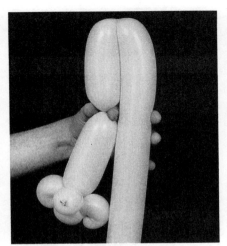

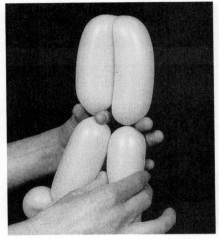

12. Straighten the two 1-inch bubbles, which are Curious George's ears, so that they look like this.

13. Next make two 4-inch bubbles and fold them down alongside the remaining length of balloon.

14. Make a third 4-inch bubble by twisting the remaining length of balloon where it meets the twist between the first two 4-inch bubbles. Do *not* secure the bubble with a locking twist.

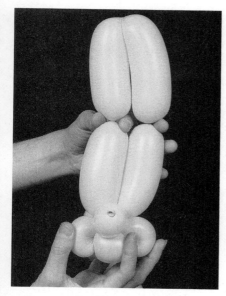

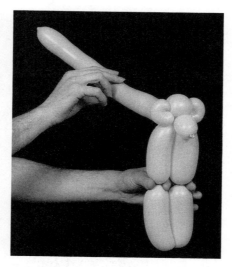

If you do not hold the middle section of 4-inch bubbles—as you see me doing in the previous photo—they should spread apart.

15. Pinch a fourth 4-inch bubble and join it, using a locking twist, with the twist beneath the head of your Curious George.

16. Twist the remaining length of balloon around so that it points straight backward from the head of your Curious George. This is what your Curious George looks like so far.

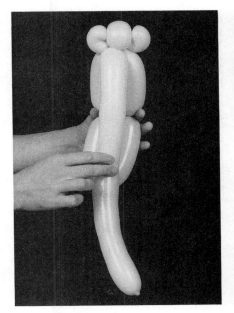

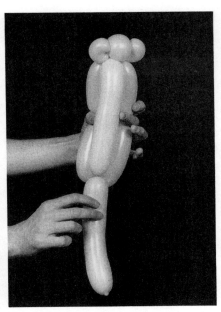

17. Stretch the remaining length of balloon down to the twist at the bottom of your four 4-inch bubbles.

18. Twist the remaining length of balloon where it meets that twist.

19. Match those two twists up and wrap the remaining length of balloon around the twist at the bottom of the four 4-inch bubbles. Push it all the way through the loop of

four 4-inch bubbles
and back around to
George's rear. This
remaining length of
balloon will be the tail
of your Curious George.

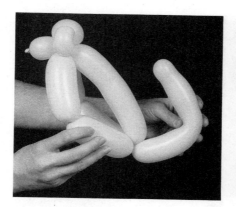

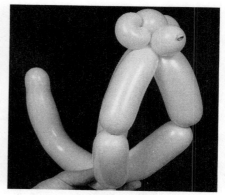

20. Roll the remaining
length of balloon back
and forth until it is
gently curved upward.

21. This is the completed
Curious George.

PUFF THE MAGIC DRAGON

This magnificent beast requires two balloons and, in my opinion, looks best if two different-colored balloons are used. The second balloon forms Puff's wings.

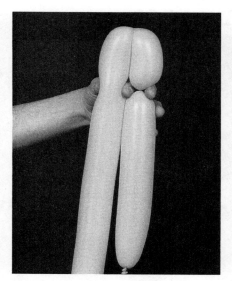

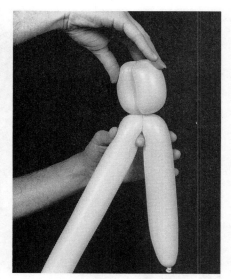

1. Inflate a balloon, leaving a 4-inch tail on the end, and tie a knot. Squeeze the balloon well, below the knot.

2. Make a 10-inch bubble, followed by a 3-inch bubble, and fold both of these bubbles down alongside the remaining length of balloon.

3. Join the bubbles with a locking twist.

130

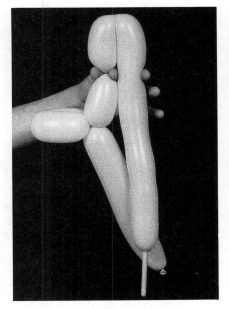

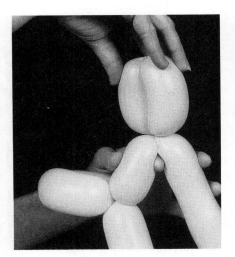

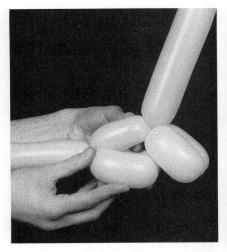

5. Join the bubbles with a locking twist.

6. Lay the first 3-inch bubble down between the second two 3-inch bubbles.

4. Make two 3-inch bubbles and fold both of them down alongside the remaining length of balloon.

 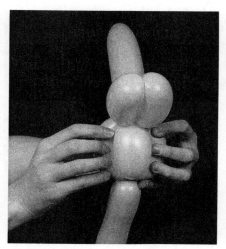 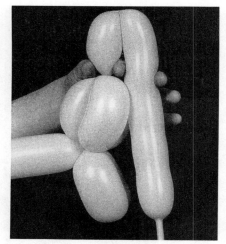

7. Gently roll the second two 3-inch bubbles around the first one.

8. At the same time, push the first 3-inch bubble until it is all the way through the second two 3-inch bubbles.

9. Squeeze the remaining length of balloon to extend the length of it just a bit, and make one 2-inch bubble. Fold this bubble down alongside the small remaining length of balloon that's left.

 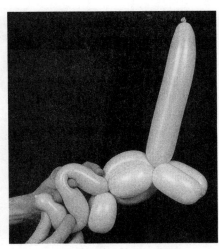 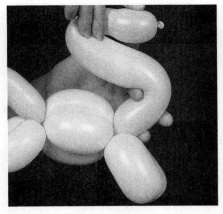

10. Join the bubbles with a locking twist at the point where the first 2-inch bubble meets the 3-inch bubbles.

11. Squeeze the remaining length of balloon until the air expands into all of it, and fold it up into an S-shape, as shown. Rock it back and forth until it holds its shape.

12. Return to the 10-inch bubble at the knot end and tug on the knot gently, while squeezing the bubble itself, to release a little extra balloon at the tip. Fold this bubble up into an S-shape as well, and rock it back and forth until it holds its shape.

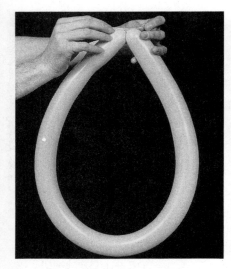

13. Inflate a second balloon until you have just a 2-inch tail on the end, and tie a knot. Bring the knot end and the tail end around in a loop and tie them together.

14. Bring this knot down to meet the body of the balloon at the point that is exactly opposite the knot. This will divide the loop in half and create two wings for Puff.

15. Grasp one of the wings and turn it around in a circle. Turn it all the way around two or three times until it locks in place.

134

16. Round out each of the smaller loops (wings) by stretching each of them with both hands.

17. Your wings will now look like this.

18. Pick up the first balloon and bring the first twist (at the base of the 10-inch bubble) to meet the twist in the middle of the wings of your second balloon.

19. Push the wings down behind the 10-inch bubble of the first balloon until the long 10-inch bubble appears to be coming directly out of the twist in the wings. You will have to really wedge the wings down into the twist.

20. Adjust the legs so that Puff appears to be standing up, and adjust the wings so that they are somewhat perpendicular to the rest of the body. This is Puff the Magic Dragon.

WINNIE THE POOH

Teddy bears are more popular than ever, but to my mind none is cuter than Christopher Robin's best friend.

137

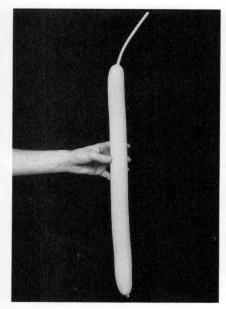

bubbles over in a loop so that the twist after the first 2-inch bubble meets the twist after the last 2-inch bubble.

1. Inflate a balloon, leaving a 6-inch tail on the end, and tie a knot. Squeeze the balloon well, below the knot.

2. Make two 2-inch bubbles, a tiny ½-inch bubble, a 1-inch bubble, another tiny ½-inch bubble, and one more 2-inch bubble. Fold all of these

138

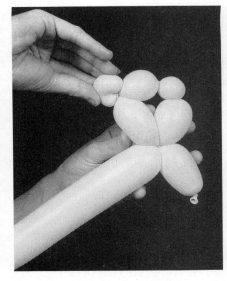

3. Hold the entire loop of bubbles and rotate it around in a circle a couple of times as shown, until the loop is locked into place.

4. Pinch one of the tiny ½-inch bubbles and pull it out from the loop just a little bit.

5. Twist it around on its ends a couple of times until it locks.

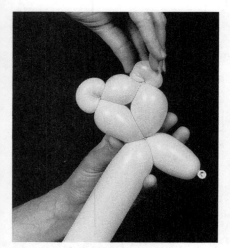
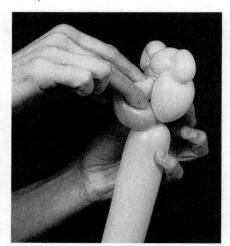
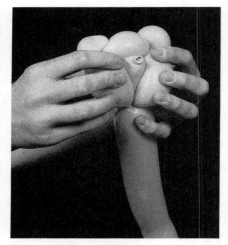

6. Repeat these same steps with the other ½-inch bubble. This is what the balloon looks like when you've twisted both ½-inch bubbles.

7. Take the 2-inch bubble at the knot end, fold it in half, and push it back, knot first, through the loop of bubbles.

8. Gently roll the loop of bubbles around the 2-inch bubble as you push the 2-inch bubble through.

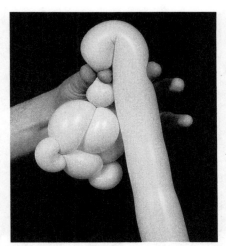

9. Push the 2-inch bubble about two thirds of the way through the loop of bubbles. Readjust Pooh's ears, if necessary.

10. Make a tiny ½-inch bubble, and pinch a 3-inch section of the remaining length. Fold this 3-inch bubble in half so that the pinch you are holding meets the twist after the tiny ½-inch bubble.

11. Twist the 3-inch bubble formed by your pinch around in a circle a couple of times until it locks in place.

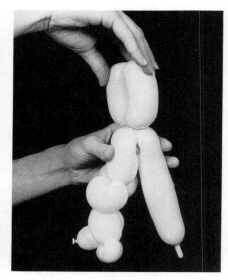

12. Repeat this procedure with another 3-inch section of the remaining length of balloon, and join it at the same place. This is what your balloon will look like when you've done this.

13. Now make two 2½-inch bubbles and fold them down alongside the remaining length of balloon.

14. Join the bubbles with a locking twist.

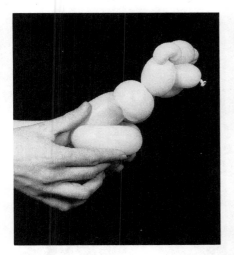

15. Lay the first 2½-inch bubble down between the second two 2½-inch bubbles.

16. Roll the second two 2½-inch bubbles around the first one.

17. At the same time, push the first 2½-inch bubble all the way through the second two.

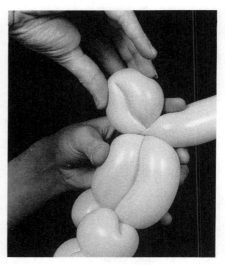

18. Turn the three 2½-inch bubbles around so that the first one is facing forward (in the same direction as Pooh's nose), and prop Pooh's arms up on his chubby body.

19. Squeeze the remaining length of balloon to extend it just a bit. Pinch a 2½-inch bubble and fold it in half.

20. Twist the folded 2½-inch bubble around in a circle a couple of times, at the point where it meets Pooh's body, until it locks in place.

the loop of bubbles that
encircles the bubble
with the knot.

21. Repeat this process
again with another
2½-inch bubble. This
will form both of Pooh's
feet.

22. Return to the knot end
of the balloon, which
will be Pooh's nose, and
give a gentle tug on the
knot to release a little
extra balloon at the tip
while gently squeezing

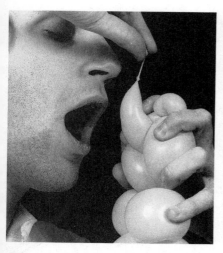

23. Still holding the knot, bend Pooh's nose up a little to give it a bit of an upward tilt. It helps to breathe a little warm air onto the balloon while you bend it upward.

24. This is Winnie the Pooh.

THE PINK PANTHER

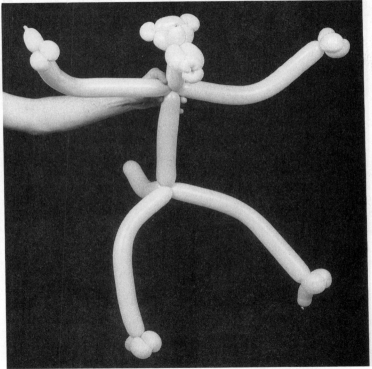

This character requires three balloons and is therefore much larger than all of the other characters in the book. He is well worth the extra balloons, though, and is a great ice breaker at parties (sit him in the corner of your couch before guests arrive).

147

all of these over in a
loop so that the twist
after your last 2½-inch
bubble meets the twist
after your first 1½-inch
bubble.

1. Inflate a balloon until
you have a 2-inch tail
on the end, and tie a
knot. Squeeze the
balloon well, below the
knot.

2. Make a 1½-inch
bubble, followed by a
2½-inch bubble,
followed by two 1-inch
bubbles, and one more
2½-inch bubble. Fold

148

3. Rotate the loop of bubbles that is formed on top around in a circle a couple of times as shown, so that it is locked in place.

4. This is what the balloon looks like at this point.

5. Pinch one of the 1-inch bubbles on top of the loop and pull it out from the loop slightly.

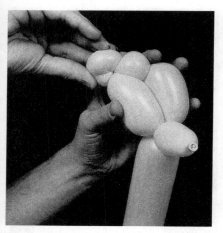

6. Twist this 1-inch bubble around on its ends a couple of times so that it stays in place.

7. Do the same thing with the adjoining 1-inch bubble.

8. Position the two twisted 1-inch bubbles so that they are perpendicular to the two 2½-inch bubbles. This is what the balloon looks like at this point.

bubbles over in a loop so that the twist after the last 1½-inch bubble meets the twist *before* the first 1½-inch bubble.

9. Make a 1½-inch bubble, followed by a 1-inch bubble, then a 2-inch bubble, another 1-inch bubble, and another 1½-inch bubble. Fold all of these

10. Holding all five of these bubbles, rotate them together around in a circle as shown. Twist them around a couple of times so that they are locked into place.

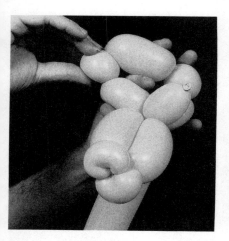
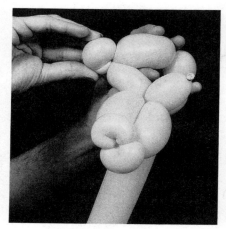
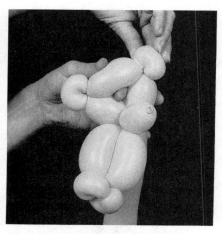

11. Pinch one of the 1-inch bubbles and pull it out slightly from the loop of bubbles.

12. Twist this bubble around on its ends, as you did in Step 6, a couple of times.

13. Do the same thing with the other 1-inch bubble.

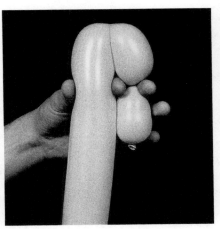

14. This is what the head of your Pink Panther looks like so far. Do any repositioning necessary to make your balloon look like the one in the picture. Set this balloon down.

15. Inflate another balloon, leaving a 2-inch tail on the end, and tie a knot. Squeeze the balloon well, below the knot. Make two 1½-inch bubbles and fold them down alongside the remaining length of the balloon.

16. Join the bubbles with a locking twist.

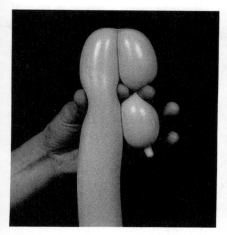

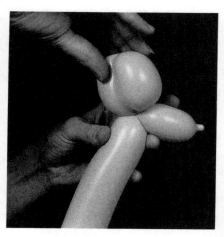

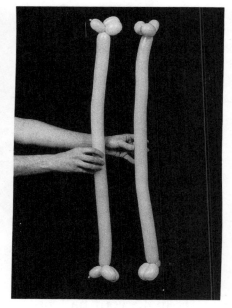

17. Squeeze the balloon well below these three bubbles to fill the entire length of the balloon. Make two more 1½-inch bubbles at the *tail* end of the balloon and fold them down alongside the length of balloon.

18. Join the bubbles with a locking twist.

19. Do the exact same thing with a *third* balloon: at *each end* of the third balloon, make two 1½-inch bubbles and join them with a locking twist. You will now have two balloons that are identical. These two balloons will be the arms and legs, respectively, of your Pink Panther.

20. Take the second balloon and place its midpoint against the remaining length of the first balloon, about three inches below the head configuration.

21. Wrap the second balloon around the length of the first balloon at this point. Wrap it tightly so that the balloons are joined and a twist is formed.

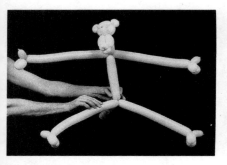

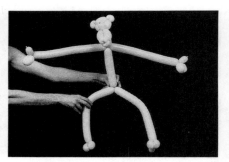

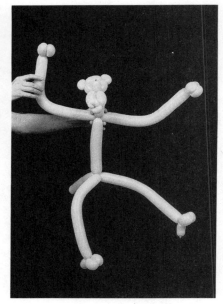

22. Place the third balloon about ten inches up from the *tail* end of the first balloon and wrap it around the first balloon as you did the second.

23. Bend the legs of your Pink Panther so that they point downward. Do this by folding them in half and rocking them back and forth until they are curved downward.

24. Bend the arms in the same manner, but so they are curved upward.

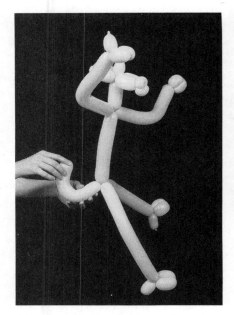

25. Bend the tail in the same fashion, so that it is curved upward.

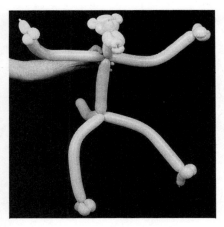

26. This is the completed Pink Panther.

ONE LAST TWIST

I'm sure you'll find many uses for your cartoon creations—they make great centerpieces for kids' parties, work beautifully as tension breakers at the office, and are a wonderful way to say "I love you" to that special someone who just happens to be a Winnie the Pooh fanatic or a Dino the Dinosaur devotee. You may also want to try making other cartoon and fictional favorites I haven't had room to include. Could Mr. Ed be modified to look more like Black Beauty? See what happens if you combine some of the face or body parts in this book with some twists of your own. Or perhaps you'd rather invent a totally new animal that isn't a cartoon but should be!

Please remember that you're likely to run out of balloons before you run out of ideas, so order more (if you can't find them locally) before you run out. And if you've fallen in love with balloon sculpting, I invite you to look for my other books: *Balloon Animals*, and *More Balloon Animals*. Happy Twisting!

MAIL-ORDER SOURCES

If you're unable to find balloons or hand pumps at your local magic, novelty, or joke shop, or if you would rather order them by mail, try one of these mail-order sources. All balloons are $15.00 per bag, postage and handling included, and come packaged 144 balloons to a bag. They are the highest-quality premium balloons available. All pumps are $6.00 each, postage and handling included. Please use U.S. currency on all orders and include an additional $3.00 postage on all orders going outside the United States.

Balloon Animals*
P.O. Box 711
Medford, MA 02155

Balloonology*
P.O. Box 301
Cambridge, MA 02238

*Massachusetts residents add 5 percent sales tax (75¢ per bag, 30¢ per pump).

Balloon Supplies
300-M Skokie Boulevard
Northbrook, IL 60062